NUMBERS AND TEMPERS

Also by Ray DiPalma

Max (1969)
Macaroons (with Stephen Shrader) (1969)
Between the Shapes (1970)
The Gallery Goers (1971)
All Bowed Down (1972)
Works in a Drawer (1972)
Borgia Circles (1972)
Time Being (with Asa Benveniste & Tom Raworth) (1972)
Soli (1974)
The Sargasso Transcries (1974)
Max/A Sequel (1974)
Accidental Interludes (1975)
Marquee (1977)
Cuiva Sails (1978)
Planh (1979)
Observatory Gardens (1979)
Genesis (1980)
Legend (with Bruce Andrews, Charles Bernstein,
    Steve McCaffery & Ron Silliman) (1980)
Labyrinth Radio (1981)
23 Works (1982)
13 Works (1982)
Two Poems (1982)
Chan (1984)
January Zero (1984)
Startle Luna (1984)
The Jukebox of Memnon (1988)
Raik (1989)
Night Copy (1990)
5 Ink Drawings/5 Poems (with Elizabeth DiPalma) (1990)
Mock Fandango (1991)
Metropolitan Corridor (1992)

Numbers and Tempers,
Selected Early Poems
1966-1986

Ray DiPalma

SUN & MOON
CLASSICS
24

Sun & Moon Press
A Program of
The Contemporary Arts Educational Project, Inc.
a nonprofit corporation
6026 Wilshire Boulevard, Los Angeles, California 90036

First published in paperback in 1993 by Sun & Moon Press

10 9 8 7 6 5 4 3 2 1
FIRST EDITION

© Ray DiPalma, 1993
Biographical information © Sun & Moon Press, 1993
All rights reserved

This book was made possible, in part, through a grant from the National Endowment for the Arts, an operational grant from the Andrew W. Mellon Foundation, and through contributions to The Contemporary Arts Educational Project, Inc., a nonprofit corporation.

Some of these poems previously appeared in *Abacus, A Hundred Posters, Benzene, boundary 2, Chiaroscuro, Grendhal Poetry Review, Ironwood, La Fusta, Multiples, Out There, Paris Review, Poetry Northwest, Roof, Sink, Sun & Moon, Talus Magazine, This, Unmuzzled Ox;* and in the books *Accidental Interludes* (Turkey Press), *All Bowed Down* (Burning Deck), *Between the Shapes* (Zeitgeist Press), *In the American Tree* (National Poetry Foundation), *"Language" Poetries* (New Directions), *None of the Above* (The Crossing Press), *Observatory Gardens* (Tuumba Press), *Soli* (Ithaca House), *Two Poems* (Awede Press), and *Works in a Drawer* (Blue Chair Press). The author would like to thank the publishers of these magazines and books. Special thanks to Brita Bergland, Charles Bernstein, Michael Gottlieb, Lyn Hejinian, Michael Lally, Douglas Messerli, Ron Silliman, and Rosmarie Waldrop.

Cover: "untitled," collage by Ray DiPalma
Reproduced by permission of the artist.
Design: Elizabeth DiPalma
Typography: Barbara Campbell

LIBRARY OF CONGRESS CATALOGING IN PUBLICATION DATA

DiPalma, Ray [1943]
Numbers and Tempers: Selected Early Poems 1966–1986
p. cm — (Sun & Moon Classics: 24)
ISBN: 1-55713-099-X
I. Title. II. Series.
811'.54—dc19
CIP 90-50332

Printed in the United States of America

Without limiting the rights under copyright reserved here, no part of this publication may be reproduced, stored in or introduced into a retrieval system, or transmitted, in any form or by any means (electronic, mechanical, photocopying, recording or otherwise), without the prior written permission of both the copyright owner and the above publisher of the book.

For Betsi

CONTENTS

ONE

Exile	12
She	14
The Privilege	16
Poem	17
Chocolates and Wine	18
Paradigm	19
The Poem	20
Fragment	21
The Daily	22
Poem	23
Poem	24
Dogs Window	25
Cologne	28
Zthonzathone	33
Lieve	34
Homage To Lichtenberg	35
Birthday Notation	36

TWO

Empire Smoke, Forgeries, Salient & The Ritz	38
Geo	41
Lever	45
Sounding	48
The Wick	49
The Bed	62

THREE

The Portion	70
Mool	71
Ode	72
Poem	75
Poem (Poem)	76
Hadrian's Lane	77
The Anecdote That Went With It	79
The Table	81
Poem	83
Orphan	84
Poem	85
Ohne	86
Chan (1)	87
Chan (2)	88
House of Morgan	89

FOUR

Say	92
Scorch	93
Mr Smileskin	94
Airliner & Hydro-matic	95
Little Mirror	96
Kinfolk	97
Oh, Au Pair	98
No Brick Window	99
Ripe Tack	100
Hoot	101
Rumours Film Island	102

Poem	103
Farm	104
Year of the Ox	105
Spook Technical	106
Gourds	107
After the Flexible Response	108
For a Drawing	109
Further	110
A Coast	111
Poem	113
The Politics of Contraband	114
Kewpie B	116
Virtuoso Peach	117
Mulberry 9	118
Eyeload and Mirrorstone	119
When Torrid Rhymes With Forehead	121

FIVE

Territory	124

ONE

EXILE

Above the tracks
a steep embank-
ment. Limestone.
Mud. Weeds. A
concrete wall
three feet high
stretches as far
as the eye can
see. Then the
traffic on the
boulevard. Homes.

Below. An iron
meadow. Tar
soaked timber.
Cans. Small
stones. More
weeds at the
back of the
filling sta-
tion near the
track's edge.

To the left
two ware-
houses. Win-
dows broken.
One wall gone.

A staircase
dangles like
the torn wall-
paper above it.
Two women eat
from a paper
bag in its shadow.

To the right
a long ramp
to a viaduct
carries the
traffic over
the boulevard.

SHE

She multiplies and divides consolation in my hands.
She cuts down my vision with her eyes.
She consumes all so that we both might want.

She stands on my heart like an island.
She allows me comfort with accusation.
She is proud of her fury.

She is my hands through the air.
She has nursed skeletons.
She is never always near.

She will pretend to die.
She chalked congealing years with great truths.
She bathed my arms with music.

She says "Leather is truth." I listen when
She strokes the linen.
She burns dandruff.

She bereaves the classic comment.
She balances salt with gold.
She stood with the hall to her back.

She always appears slowly.
She is not my child.
She has a face for children.

She has translated stone. When we do not speak
She quips with the shuddering walls.
She walks in my sleep through my dreamless shiftings.

She knows wisdom is stolen.
She is behind you.
She has breasts of a stranger woman.

She crossed the beach beneath the sun.
She cupped the ocean between her legs as
She left me.

THE PRIVILEGE

A gift
for the few
of the few

who
never had
to ask.

POEM

I sleep in this

I wear this only
  to keep me warm

I wear this in the street

This goes on my back
  only when I am
  alone and cold

I go here only
  to pass the time
I go there only
  to find the time

I make a purchase
  to take my time

I walk
  here and there
  for the same reason

I eat   I don't eat

Patterns occupy my desires

The answer is next

CHOCOLATES AND WINE

London opens on a narrow balcony
the ridiculous walker heads for Goswell Road
He has listed his favorite streets
on a small piece of vellum
pinned to his sleeve

>Haunch of Venison Yard
>Shavers Place
>Bear Alley
>Weirs Passage
>Jacobs Well Mews
>Great Maze Pond
>Smyrks Road
>Old Swan Lane
>Strype Street
>Bacchus Walk
>Frying Pan Alley

The eternal guest   cold face against
the bookshop window

this city was below the sound of his feet
as he stopped and healed the purple grumbling

a bell in the wave

PARADIGM

I would make an extravagance of an example
Concluding in the peculiar
All influential expectations and introductions.
Turn to wood. Allow for my hand.
Admire by dint of provocation
Results so symptomatic of the bizarre
They only make for good manners. I am
Going around with a code of upheavals
Meant to languish in the quotidian.
I overlook the trickling polarizations
The simultaneous degrades with its further drownings.
I do not have to begin to feel I can find
You anywhere. You are always ready with the match
Taking over the nod. Fear in the mouth
Where a sum total accommodates an empty hand
Pointing at the fire.

THE POEM

So vital. So unimportant.
And after that you laugh.

"Where it belongs after all…"

As much of life as I may safely confuse
Falls from your hands. The escape is travel
Exercising its belief in qualities isolated
By sleep and best left out of earshot.
Too much sense for one chance to confuse the law.

Birds strike out
Negotiating conduct negotiating
Mercy and sullen movements like guests who
Bring silence to the grooves.
The boy with blue hair
In the moonlight
Is too modest. Page across the light he sits before…
It's the things getting out that worry us.

FRAGMENT

sooner or later the sun cracks rebecca
sooner or later the sun hits
and not much is left of her
and cabbage the dog

misery is singing its pennies on the horizon
and rebecca of the sleek mechanics kisses
her knuckles

sick rebecca
of the tick and lop
inches through the dry foliage
cashes in her stockings

1001 sharks the sun
re-b re-b re-b
hawks and sharp stones

THE DAILY

On the open door the prey
ajar agreed on vast as what
could be another coupon

Taken through all alphabets
the letter shadows into the spoon
special as some other tool to be reckoned with

Withdrawn as the special recognized
by the air today size lives the life
of a lock not about to vanish

I see you in your green hat
Hatching a bargain out of prophecy
made in another pleasant authority and noise

POEM

In danger of which
all other things are
part matter part remark

Good morning
and afternoon floundering
in its own extravagance

In danger of ending
and none too soon to light
the modest impression we have of light

No candle no wick no taper
torch or rotting log
we can forgive the head its buryings

The clasp of resources
to the ebbing image
this too is still an elevation

Mood needs a sampler now and again
now and again
blue sitting forgiving the dark

victims especially

POEM

From morning straight
Time reading white
Mouths more formal than success
While against your fitting
Pulse coils and fiber branches

The faster we bow
The edge
And how alternative the week's word
Locates
Falls still facing the fill

Return
Turn to the numerous
And sleep
The tall grass
Moving its animal

DOGS WINDOW

Zinn: Head down I must translate
        The work and worry.
        Who can write the long sentence?
        Who can't?
        Who can endure it?

Maaf: Impartial from the room,
        Forehead to the sky
        I stroll the white lawn.
        Never a night sky.
        Never an empty street.

Zinn: Classic parody, witty negation.
        What's there to want?
        Mid-progress built in.
        O my chest is full
        Of hesitation!

Maaf: I have drawn a line
        To last season's window.
        I don't look for the sun.
        I don't care to see the cars.
        It's the path alone appeals.
        I can hear it. Working souvenir.

Zinn: Canny judgements notice me.
      My need's through with its energies.
      Am I done for?
      How the future cuts me with its logic!
      Can I be asleep? Masterful?

Maaf: I listen and eternity feints.
      Shame could be a friend now
      In what seems the season for it.
      Daggers broken. Blood caresses us.
      The less whimsical beard reasons
      I guess.

Zinn: Half know their idyll.
      Found soon enough.
      But I am here with my
      Green ink for harking back.

Maaf: Walking out on memories
      For a sleep. Warm stone
      Follows the profile.
      Brighter accident!
      Give the man a cigar!
      No one ever said that to me.

Zinn: Who liked the laugh?
      Who likes the laugh
      Shoots the lion.
      Big brain! Interesting ideas
      Always seem the same.

Maaf: Zinn Zinn Zinn Zinn!
      It's volume stops this tune!
      Stops it with a stab
      In the spectre's back.

Zinn: The work and worry
      Instead of the brick and song
      Eh?

Maaf: Instead of.

COLOGNE

The paintbrush smothered the slowly ascending scream.

The Steubenville profit has a medium size pulpit.

The excavations of last December turned purple.

The floating accommodations were signed by public citizens.

The laughter rests in your hands tomorrow.

The Memorial Seams shouldn't be pursued without police.

The turnpike necks are undreamt of.

The little fool starched the charms with Connecticut dispensers.

The stone or apple hit the deer.

The chalet by your trousers is owned by American Express.

The fractured wings shook loose the fireweed.

The left hand is best considered so.

The pile of brick dust has a boggy resonance.

The pooch loves snow when it's catty-corner to a briquette.

The past failures and successes sound like needles.

The girl from California has long legs.

The portulacas are in a boisterous muddle.

The carpenter has a brother named Eric.

The porcelain china on the wet steps is wet.

The blouse in the corridor was kissed.

The lieutenant broke the shutters and let in the darkness.

The chef at Tivoli's ate a tomato sandwich with poor posture.

The bird swooped like an airplane lands to avoid birds.

The Chinaman put his hand in your mouth.

The crotchety farmer cemented his tree.

The lapels avoided criticism.

The young communist brought a great sense of relief.

The alarm clock abandoned the coast.

The sewer was subjunctive.

The closed door opened.

The planet Mildred exposed a crushed snail.

The helicopters canvassed the aluminum funeral.

The mouth sometimes provides a regular routine.

The finish line was invited to dine with high society.

The more interesting bread was falsified and intolerant.

The clerk gathered speed on Tuesday.

The belly conferred with the encyclopedia.

The fenders turned tail and flipped through a pamphlet.

The patrol glanced at his humility.

The antennae were half-way up the Madam.

The charities pinballed in the nude.

The skate key is in the creme de menthe from Paula.

The lounge died of thirst.

The creature on your hip has a job in Wisconsin.

The funnel went to Pittsburgh for surgery.

The Cheese Anthology won't fit in your watch band.

The smoker broke his wrist.

The grass was illuminated by three old fireflies.

The parrot who sells newspapers now shines shoes.

The Denver sheets were brought to Alfred the Drudge.

The comma is bent on suicide.

The calendar lurks.

The photo of Proust you gave me is now 63 years old.

The phalanx is sold on theology.

The symbols for cabaña and bully are beach ball and beach.

The bleeding handles were excused from tarnish school.

The vestigial spittle had creased the cows.

The dinky twitch you called rhythm fenced the butterscotch.

The disguised oversimplifications were sort of funny.

The brass breast was a partial failure.

The rug fell asleep over natural history.

The commandos have money worries with Veronica.

The Sanhedrin cooked an apple stew for Bruce.

The bald girl held my hand.

The piss ant tickled the barnacle.

The Sadduccees were hardassed but easily committed to memory.

The third lady from the left has been known to limp.

The castanets were holding down the fort.

The senator was tempted.

The drunk, for example, said the bulletins were a commercial hit.

The revolver even went to the birthday party in Maine.

The decline of Christmas as a banana is very good.

The curtain choked the pellet.

The Elizabethans rarely went to the jungle.

The prairie schooner is damp.

The jolly duck shot the ostrich and the kangaroo.

The vicious attack progressed handsomely.

The luncheonette was crowded with Serbians.

The sleeper scratched the thunder.

The extenuating pillars were late for the drumroll.

The seeds will guffaw the ambulance.

The tropical deltas are without valentines.

The more aggressive infatuations get a trowel.

The appetite sparkled with information concerning the sky and lakes.

The new window won't change your memory.

ZTHONZATHONE

Where we point
In the name of love

We are found
Pointing

In the next
Direction

Some things
Cannot be

Compressed

LIEVE

This is the terrible
botanical panic-stricken
stasis of Keats

This
is not

This is the simple physical
irritation of Schopenhauer

This
is too

These are the rare periods
of relative ease
and corrosion of heart

This and *this*
and *this* are not

HOMAGE TO LICHTENBERG

To tolerate the village idiot
But not everybody
That's chemistry

BIRTHDAY NOTATION

On September 27, 1855, Tennyson read *Maud* aloud to a group of friends—Robert and Mrs. Browning, Mrs. Browning's sister Arabella (Barrett), and Dante Gabriel and William Michael Rossetti. Sitting unobserved in a corner, Dante Gabriel Rossetti made a rapid but good portrait of Tennyson, which he later gave to Browning. According to W. M. Rossetti, Tennyson did not know of the picture, at the time or afterward.

When *Maud* had been read through (with Tennyson interrupting himself frequently to comment on individual passages), Browning read *Fra Lippo Lippi*, and the party broke up at two-thirty A.M.

TWO

EMPIRE SMOKE, FORGERIES, SALIENT & THE RITZ

China island dream
   dragging blot centuries
suddenly smoke
   boxes rather close
Virginia determination
   echo drowned luncheon
dyspeptic lodgings cigarette
   electricity put into words
and always in silence
   taken color
reminiscent climax for evil
   sanctuary driven
common flames louder glance
   temperate dancing
books claret shake pose boots
   hire steps bird angle
wagon pity

   matters eight occasion
unequal glorious coin line
   set matters loan pier
sterling abbey post amber
   merit thread
doorway grace lemon cull
   conditions back shop duke from kicking
green stifle measures vein lob
   bas-relief cork tomb cardinal

about sunset air
    sixteen figs and two small loaves
dense finches
    rattling craters
broad bracelets of blue beads
    envy of the rain
storm bay
    anchors famine rocks coral proper lagoon

cogent arrow
    porous strata accurate mill roots
great certain registers genius
    blister hill pry speech
cosmic matrix
    a tribal fold in the other
court marine wafer flame
    savant beat
skids plateau
    wide timid basking
husks sham cries arc lane
    image gable as attitude
gates limbo
    does he epitome sort fumes
gusts ranger moment pole
    bulk mere field zones
cave droll

    flint pylons
daylight board
    alcohol sand current
shepherd garden deuce
    in beg whisper mount

just dull wedge lord
    buoyant neon
chronic kindle motif
    stippled vizier tambourine
vicar bone vents torpor
    gazette canal
rain crow walking the load
    ticket lips
turf lace
    buckle chin
pressure mole
    shed berry

pairings fever junction
    warp shoot
tropical vapor pulse
    cool blown dark hovel
chant rind
    grey beams dome chimes
mandolin corners
    half bronze clear shore
coup manor check
    festival inches
palms and pastels
    brass vials and sector
aureole gate
    bubble wire
atmosphere dart
    sly garlic and caporal
after soft sketches

GEO

Nothing west beyond
the Canary Islands
along an irregularly
built street turning
to the left
square pocket mathematically
irresistable gold poured
into some hollow
sticks treated as
a piece of
kindness with respect
to the zodiac
and the cycles
of change keys
the profounder the
completer keeping track
of seven planetary
pointers eyes on
months wood glass
silk a depressed

weather color every

now and then

I tell her

a dream I've

had so she

can have something

to analyze Nile

China compelled to

believe the number

ladder If addressed

as If not

mythograph translators in

the song grotto

a fabric of

charts here is

a piece of

game long since

known to us

as the assumption

when I think

it over however

I am wrong

in treating it

as a greater

imposition at the

bottom it imposes

obligations on me

which I must

be prepared to

make sacrifices to

fulfill anthropos and

sophist a dynamism

in an ordinary

idea mind more

marked satisfaction recognized

dull eyes set

fast tea for

garlic by violence

by great leading

the effects and

properties of ideals

and standards dim

memory only failure

in the face

of privilege can

dislodge common and

direct or what

the horizontal obtains

LEVER

lies
kin
stands

fills

one
follows
and is
seduced

trick track
the end
less
    calculation
echo and
rhythm
feeling
less being
total presence
rhythm
walks
in turn
movement
tracks

come on
clear traces
while
the one
hand
treasure
contains
a light
it does
not
cherish
edge and
weight
from hand
to hand
shifting
knot
hostile
expectation

locks
solid
the space
an overflow
gains
in manner
darkens
but cannot
move
vessel stone
nothing

outside
its walls
instinctive
one
      is original
building
even
during
the ebb

SOUNDING

Pressing about with a spring
pulling a small pattern detaining passive
measure passing demeanor sight's balance equine
divided walk to say amaze the basic
a weight outward against any extent
specifically native by all sorts of devices
the stone model buoyant and peculiar
among the living once directed memory
the past power that veneers the sources
always spoken in terms of the whole song
directed the pitch and angle waiting
patiently opening on an array of people
dressed for the day but those still
standing say he features ideas answering
the thinkers a natural process that permits
no empty synthesis or vapid constraint
a cage without hazard for droll bastards
without the aboriginal hum chaos at the nape
the old mood facing cameos for detainees
mezzotints of an idea logged in the privacy
of the dinner table what this not large enough
to contain it technologic and pretending selection
a few words over a mile long languor poised
under the elephant library of false economy
mutual illusion in a room filled with smoke
rancor granted for the small target
accurate decorum for the puny spirit
injunction granted and pause ploughed under
winds temper and answer to hold the signal
for the habit opinion obtains

THE WICK

Light over
thumb
immaculate bars

the reasoned
presence
secrets

and white walls
pointing mirrors
we allow in

skin and numbers
gathering attention
the hoop

or finding
and articulating
the unit

in the variety
the horizon
fixing

the angle
of gravity
100 oxen

to the muses
for the dovetail
then a pattern

of contemplation
its traceries
mystic comfort

the sun
powering
water

arc-ing
the resolve of space
out of function

unposed eye
unformulated
situate

individualizing
contagion
facing outward

sediment
detail
frontier

proportion
ranks
common as blind

structure
stricken
stuck

analysis
reflective
swindle

what's wrong
with the same blood
hands over the sleeper

for coherent
magic
a tenuous grasp

shouts no pain
where no pain
shouts or time locks

where the hand burns
no sleep
category rhythm

next grasp
comes up
quiet

between the flows
pivots
and sharpens

if consequence
is decision
blame waits

and the dance
brings priorities
this dance

spontaneous stages
of the grid epic
efficacies

caught avenue
reflect surface
kingdom of the tongue

the tooth
splits the contour
into distance

and none
the less
still phantom

syndic of minus
gesture of task
dragging affections

through the catastrophe
smiling eyes
shut

meticulous and
compliant vagaries
make yonder

dark to light
light to dark
as or

and the lines return
limber for the strategies
hyperextensive

appliant
blind witness
with a fine feeling

uproar memory
links beyond
speech into fractions

exchange
on the mark
shouldering

the apparatus
the wing
the floor its climate

rigmarole
receptive
labelled sense

the quantum
of grave
isolation

is not
synthesis
but slow

outward
flight
shadow and light

not where
things normally
happen

but where
you
can sleep

never mind
rising to
the occasion

amid
the madness
an annoyance

this dream
figures
in the corner

to corner
slow
outward

flight
not the gloss
of directive

the tongue's hem
moon clear
burns

tension
a quiet
blot

the path in
for these
are better sources

brittle
mannerist
piecework

broken
on science rock
lodging taste

wedged
can when with
a stone

but no
famed
transformation

but
no
but or

and the face
to the mind
restored

narrow streets
in the faces
level

dignity gaped at
a cliff
to a cage

old words
old words in a pile
of fifteeners

in one
any one the paradise
of cool waters

burns down
takes
the measure

k to x
even there
squares to an end

who has seen this
and how painted
painted

now
hands over
light over thumb

stares
it does
little else

or waiting
for a signal
lights to blink

a parrot on a
postcard inscribed
Lux Orfeo

not
proper
moonlight

candid shadow
chorus companion
sufficient particular

the qualities
not just the light
touch

ice and smoke
at the top
of the root

level with
untranslated
forget

the humid wink
of the sad
tumescent mandarin

the complicated
what passes through
resonant

fixed
not over the shoulder
transfixed

zigzag as the suspect knot
the knot the just
delay

certain count
neat configurations
blue sky

as and as
wand and
night conjecture

two by two the two
and two as I
how everything

into the faces
lights
and vowels abide

the back
confident
celebration

as few
say taut
delights

the dog and I
see a cloud
banner

and bird
in the movement
of a scorpion's tail

the horse
is still running
the eye unbruised

goes on
the reach forward
facing back

actors
surrounding
fingers

the claim
of reason
here to peer into

what
to go on
not to go on

the slight hand
over the oval
is this form

tranced
is this
one where's

the answering oval
where's
the pen

tubes
pipes
and bellows

the grain
and the stars
sit

quiet
the rest
do with

THE BED

Dark o'clock
Be solid maybe inside
But adequately
Dead one by the sequence

And tumble
Light
Presses daylight
Brick to waver brick

To build or boundary
You'd think
Come closer
And the voices

All so flat
Half-fallen off
Hunting the careless
In the parade

How can white be
The moon looks down
And turns
Thin and bitter

So I'll go back
We'll reach
Every back and mirror
Turning dangerous

Between the nostrils
Earning a little borrowed air
Right right proportions
Crabbing and opaque between yawns

A first coat a
Second coat or
Are you hearing things
Perfect decoys

Like the tug of yellow
Like neighboring thumb and finger
Yours and hers
Mine and yours or not yours and hers

Delicate and unperturbed
A slithering irridescence
That would be inscrutable
Were it not fact

Wan clever minutely natural
Nearly perfect
Gone to seed like columbine
Nearly perfect

As when all the lights
Go out you can walk backwards
With perfect impunity
And say so

How clever to be invisible
A length of iron pipe in your pocket
Your voice a shadow
Behind your teeth

An inheritor
Pumping the space with decimals
Approach the cultivating claw
Brother

Where four billion years
Of nature two million dollars
One million miles and thirteen
Hours inspire chat

There there now the coincidences
Back to back the convincing quirks
Make for the calmly circumspect
A perfect garden in which to dance

Moves winding meticulous
As buds twist a branch
Light dismantling a wave
Memory copying touch

A surge and violent hush
Composed aurora but can't trust
The wind now though it's a great response
I prefer to the ripeness of words

Passing through a perfect frame
Of backlit steam reds greens blues
Pausing just long enough
To take the measure

The lines the four corners
Embody memory large and impersonal
No better to say
The stiff angles of deflection

No better
To say no better to say
Comes and goes but just so far
Purpling as it happens

Amicably solemn
The remote terrors of proportion
Confide the raw
Dreaming the intricate

Unaccompanied
The word of a stranger
Nostrums and random exceptions
Inclination or opinion

The fastidious analogue
The ballad and the prejudice
Intense solitude
Wilderness to wilderness

The coin or the kindness
A high tambourine
Shrugged shoulders
Spectacle volunteer

Peculiar to certain orders
Like the assassin
Broken imperfectly on a conviction
But enthralled by a mere prospect

Dependable phantoms
The song after the music
Not the chase but
The paint drying

Grammar is black
Syntax is starch
Hello Reverend X
Hello Reverend Y

A thin black line
The collar of the coat turned up
Evertheless I liked the way mere touch
Could make the beads spin

Make me feel tribal
In my secure sense of objectivity
Like a great ritual vessel
Lost but floating free

Stock water disguise functions
You pay for the freedom
To come with me
Water and brain chemistry

Wine brandy apples rosin
Cork paper toys perfumes
Oil pitch tar oak pewter
Linen silk lace salt gin

Good loam soil weighs
Eighty pounds a cubic foot
Clay carries a strong negative electric
Charge so things cling to it

THREE

THE PORTION

This part
is mine
for me

this part
of that
is for you

but not
you and
you alone

this part
of that
and close

to the edge
crust
not conclusions

MOOL

No pretending the far thought

or ponder's briar and cobble

a nostalgia for barbarism

setting forth the grievance

ODE

      Distance in the breeze
       a line a thousand miles long
     iridescent grandiose subjective
the work of observation
    through the roof
        expenditures of subtle memory
     should consider travel
  not the discrete disintegration
    of an ample design
        fluctuations of influence wooed
    tropical speed invited
       temperament blanked by allusion
a minutely organized system in the ruins
   snaking through daydream and sleep
      now a window now a sentiment now a season
a navigator's privilege not coercion
or the distillate of false confidence
nuanced by the imagined authority of effort
or private satisfaction
   overpowering the shared province of fact
   extended not recognized
   vanity and many marvels
     how adequate the intimate
    definite attention located
     eyeful purchase on what
      is chewed and what is
     burnt off completely
    leisure's analytical contrivance
      a severed head

         remembering the tense
          of some modest isolation
        edging through coincidence
        unnoticed subtleties repeated
           shifts to carry measure
         that that and that
             where speakers play
           set apart by scrutiny
      the private burden and
        its dreaming emphasis
          the reach of the uninhabited
            how elusive how generous
             the uninstructed remark
           as the breeze reminds impulse
           curling into the light
              as too many means
              in sight done and displayed
        curiosity shut down
      alert to pass unnoticed
           by a very complicated route
             one wondered one note
distinct phases suspending the vapor
throwing the horizon into relief
      red red black and blue
         a lustre never penetrated
       a calm rustic synthesis
         under a composite sky
             plumes of smoke vanished dialects
         weaving the shallows with music
           resemblance standing by
               distrustfully good natured

attenuated considerations of the upper air
susceptible to the yardstick of treatment
    the singular stepped apart
    shrugs imperfectly parried
    the etude of frisk and feint
    anticipating a share of its own response
    the consequence of mound builders
    in a meadow before a storm
      the sport of currents

POEM

Face to face and in the face
These are the misleading susceptibilities
Tensed and caressing in a mixture
Nothing human but shaped by light

Caught then a word whistling up to spend
Or to spend some time together
A somber brush or melancholy blossoming
Through the curious to the vehement attitude

A lethal parallel right through say
The hypnotist's lie and the long and short of the song
Contriving chance or suppressing an abrupt notion
Expressionless retorted the reflective bread

Garb and garbled charms contrast shrill strokes
Top down and across to the right or up from the left
To the top no higher but to the upper right
No plateau no reach just the parallel reflected

Forbearing the given and its little distance
Then a vapor anticipating the spectacle
The suspect modulated obtaining silence with a gesture
Fresh points of platitude rising in columns of black smoke

Stranger than questionable or what is amplitude
In more than probable crouched in a corner
Some restless scrutiny confounds the offensive modesty
Liking the rule that corrects the emotion

POEM (POEM)

Perspective flickers
the barriers inexplicable
as always and the way in
the way out discreet but
changing the hymn in the
shifts engendering the isolate
so tooled to and geared in
to a grace of phase that skill
just stares and instinct calms

At any moment I don't have a place
but remember to my credit some pleasure
or thump of fortune the sun's rays
through a timber-framed phantasmagoria
lulling suspicion or turning the wheel
to the place to surprise an able impulse
incapable of speech and under control
a stab transfixing the lithe and imperturbably
calm aspect of the rare or once disdained

Or and if at any moment I find the place
and forget the thump of fortune now called
a judgement alternately auguring tone and
the headlong ruse too tested for instinct
and measured even to tremble like a notion
forking the tact and in the throat turns
back the graceful proportions of an alternative
memory enhanced inclining made effective as
hope or a grip or a good opinion charmed

HADRIAN'S LANE

What fills the whisper and
all want fragments why along to check
the short page what your convictions
this is shudder and this is antenna mail

Not from here like a lot of wax lost wax
in fact misplaced the emptying the song
finishers indexing the aces ring phone
and circulate here and there a wave or

Something much harder for sleep like dance
rendering the up trace or cross cowers
for a bow makes for silence the big
polar wag the shift heads to roam

The volume cores the abject delirium of
capital the compressors fill from middle out
with a weird blue light too much focus on
the night too few stars a big chunk of it

How inert the dutiful to stare right into
how inflected as it were to bend or shape
from a straight to a narrow this is the way
from however to how best you hound the path

Remote air logic to take the measure
from ether logic to casual fulcrum block
can it go up and out into that remoteness
strain to the then and then and then softer flight

Well it seems there's a drubbed restraint
makes for the go road and empty bit of hum
nice target maybe or perspective's arena
squared in the calm wake of looksee

And then has a gander for totals
sprints the high street and makes for the fog
number shadow clue and mark it from rut to rut
frost heaves apprehend then the gallery of trees

Appetites tug at the argument and mood freight
a brain nab for smooth talk addlers of give go
all so much carbon the think's gummed
coordinated like currents but breaks the ankle

Obdurate wince to scuff the instanter
the junk prick cracking the ellipse
so now it's how you say an oval and hung
in a corrosive pose you get at it prying

THE ANECDOTE THAT WENT WITH IT

The long reaches of the street.
Everything in order.
Pull it.

First the food.
Then the politics.
Not so much anymore.

Maybe. Maybe
Not. Maybe not.
Fails to flatter the prospects.

Folds against the seams.
It tightens off.
Blood flows.

The opposite shore the
Consequence of its own
Notion of righteous scrutiny.

It's what's done. It's
Just what's done.
That's all that's it.

But a reasonable solitude
Is a matter of months
Not a new man proposal.

The old symphony story
Looking right into the light
Is ink. Specters.

The edges of the shapes of color.
A chrome weasel a loam curve.
Vapors and self-fix hoodoo.

There they are moving slowly.
Stalks gathering. Stalkers.
Sunlight.

He was talking about the essential
Language only reminding us of pain.
Tale told tale heard tale told heard.

THE TABLE

Not wide but a wing
Balancing a sphere
Dissolving in a reward
Of fog—conversation's
Beard of light

Interest reaches
And there are large white plates
Indicators
Wintering
Tall glasses and a bowl of salt

Cold but agreeable
The place for it
The abstract agriculture of stones
The extended hand and
Bent neck of the earnest pilgrim

Just a hand around the curve
Once enough
and to believe
An accident
In the dark

POEM

Light follows light
Shadows ripple calm
As a bowl of fruit
Inventing the curve

A passion for measurement
Traced on wall and ceiling
A remote and agitated pattern
And from a crouch asking—just
To ask "Why is the floor moving"

A perspective, just a perspective
The small bells of cleft and moment
Percussive resonance brings for harmony
The strummed depth in out in and words to
Hard lines like impacted resin

ORPHAN

Half a holiday with an arm in the wall
An inordinate number of reproaches

Double foreground
Ancient Scotland or a farm upstate

Traffic in utterance
Alms in the clothes moaning clothes

Not ideas projects
Written arguments five thousand miles of leaves

Ten in the light
Twisted and tailored for ten

So here's this now I was told this
An elaborate frontier emerges

Radio shoes plumbing fireworks
Tension privilege freight

POEM

I think he thought
He could push it
A little further
Out and maybe through
Pretend some choices
And spite some earlier
Ideas and intervals
Organize the graces
The tripped shadows
Across the blank pages
Of a half-opened book
Images in a 5000 year
Old mirror bitter and
Brief a false creature
But always at it and
Looking through all
The evidence never
Squinting but never
Trusting the told
Colors but the edges
Where the complex
Of predictions had
Run to mere fact
The torn margin
The horizon an inscription
Emptying the earliest dream
The first hill is a shoulder

OHNE

Push power. The range. Remarkable gear. The turn. Tight bait the ears. The brevity of first convenience. Essayed. Thrifty light. Paper. Gypsy oil. Circle semi-circle. Machines. Thistle braid. Kicked slate—that for the mark. And now the mark is missing. For balance a wedge. The contact of work. Punkt. Zero the sitter. Line from the eyes. East to west in a barrel. The darkness quite suited to speaking clearly. There it was. The perfection of leisure—darkness. Not a tunnel as before but an enclosed cylinder. Worthy. Now rotation is health. Not my heels in my ears as in the past. What a federation of latitudes for echo after echo measures me. Crisp banners of sound. Ribbed. Baffled. Palming the mark for a while then still. The mark new each and every time then still. Along it. Then again. And come to it, all of it, as others before me. Palming the mark. The edge of measure not its fullness. Never that. Or perhaps not until now. But that would come. But to speak of it as others before me had scratched some few signs here and there in the warm light. Elegiac in anticipation. The waiting. That's where it came from. That tone of subdued consequence. This is not what we came for but are sad and lyric in our presumptions. Strummers. But this is how I whistle where there are no corners. No bung for my tail. This is wisdom. All colors for my treadle. For memory fragments of spite. Sharp though infrequent. How memory works it. Placates the turns.

CHAN (1)

Disappearing into new efforts

East
a memory

Gold, dried glue, paper
The citizen's record

Thersites
on the School of Pergamum

    chewed by warnings and omens
Songbird cicero

From a spyglass
The vantage

Red runners bring hummingbirds

Horses run in the date palms

Flares

CHAN (2)

Because there are
some things
I cannot say
You say them with me

Marking the path
history's stone

opposite
the cold sphere
unpainted
drawing light
and no air
gathering
rigged for breath
pipes rope tube

small stone
some the size of loaves

HOUSE OF MORGAN

Fortunes

and black capitals

if it slips the bit
you've got to get off

clutching
the walk along
is better

than ride behind for
what falls off the wagon

non ce'marchandies peressables

An ancient system
and Cato
and his scowl and hiss
comes next

A word in your ear
stinkmouth

dollars
the long word

saying what never
might be *read*

just balance

caper and balance

folding

no domestic detail
worked into image

lines from the predicted
get
loud

FOUR

SAY

Say what
you mean
shoes pointed
at the music
no diversion
in silence
or stiff talk
but an astounding
plan
nothing wasted
locking up
the psychic hunch
in pride's economy

SCORCH

Some resonance beyond the occasion

never mind the result

two women and a man the locked door

tolling in the stew

MR SMILESKIN

Perhaps
the moment
isn't right
Remember
Uriah
burning the pouch
The carrot man
wringing his hands

AIRLINER & HYDRO-MATIC

A man in short hair
Camel hair coat
Black suede shoes
Tell my horse
Astounding Stories
Steer the Lancia
Out in the direction
Of the rhythm and bells
Hot gun cooled down
Lace and red coals
Glint off the speaking tube
It still took him
Three minutes to open the door
Bambino figlio mio

LITTLE MIRROR

Play the great
tunes and move
the moves for-
get the commerce
walk like a man
remember where
the bee lands

KINFOLK

Boober, he's the one

Tub and shay

Barnboard hay and hammer

Bale my foot

Boober, he's the one

OH, AU PAIR

A pair
of paired
pear halves

NO BRICK WINDOW

Big superstitious wedge lodged
In the pattern
Bad blood drab sphere full of ponder
Origins molars clothes moon marrow
Baking in the cap

RIPE TACK

Keel's echo small stagger
Float ridges load
Of old oaken stupors

Cool gravity local worth
Small room a cell a cabin
balanced in guilds

Scrawl of fields
acre and banner
flower and arrow

HOOT

Wrapped in waves and rays
graces and the recitation
of wonders six and seven
at a clip a decorative Giant
in corduroy cue the rigid tides
compute the bud worry the turf
bark pinions and yodel bone

RUMORS FILM ISLAND

Walkie-talkie triangle
All pastel no tones
Short blunt points
To put it across
Crack muting steam
The giant beaten
Column column column
A sort of hallway
Publicity fragments
In the filament
Discreet palm cloud
Paper blocks maps hoards
The public face

POEM

desert
horse penetrating the frontier
small hard-footed short back
lumbar fusion shapes the continent

FARM

morning rides
horses
hurtling machines

dogs and
other dogs
noise and company

moving on
more or less true
macabre coping

no answer
for many years
free rhythm for

bonus tonk
great red shadows
on the boards

YEAR OF THE OX

As in medias res so concerned to say this
is the first hand not the second the reduced
by mathematical pattern dislodged by accident
or the ear on the bus or train not luggage handler
luck in the lost and found or this spare
disclosure of the circle's wide turn
the square's trick angle turning the breath outward
then not the texture's look almost perfect its
cut shine white yellow green the bright
cool sky light using the gate mixing the grain

SPOOK TECHNICAL

Bald chilly copy out of the bone sheen

glib as glib french squirming in the rattle

A complex phrenology of particulars

sewn into the hum

A sad echo a stifled hoot

Keening from the mud radio

Must be biological traction

GOURDS

The easy gray square in a street language
Deals the medium a glued edge and climate of cheek
The spell in a bag of smoke
What would happen if the spell scratched
And rested—the secret frantic index of squalls

Credentials and a million cigarettes maybe
A true and thorough moment with the grace of sidestep
Gone up in the rocket in the talk of lyric
Decoding the surgical moments this lingo
Cuts along—the position of the sun a simple act

News like hair or that special electric giggle
In the hand writing its lone famous index of rhythms
Chesthigh in noontime reprieves because a series
Nourishes after all and crazy fingers can probe
The throat aches—tender songs on the hog biscuit tongue

Put away the xylophone we're going to explore
Some underground art all over your nose or just inches
Away lodged in the bright glimpse the sweat in your eye
Affords once you get your feelings straight
We'll gather under the collapsed dome—ride the verb jack

AFTER THE FLEXIBLE RESPONSE

The tremendous pillow solos of philosophy
Beckon the nonchalance of the posthumous
Plaintive and very ancient laughter
Replaces discussion and its pendulum languor
Gray archival light encourages sleep
Full of humid distances and delicate architectures of risk

Solemn tensions build a mound in the eye
A heap of grandeur to abide in the years of straggle
Imagine the pretty urges and the speculative days to come
Passing ingrown and perennial under a vast and altering frost
The monster of rescue intrigued by the broken space

These are nights with a cracked approach
Unlocked and floating, circling the trees
The sentry moan in the warp and curve
Imitates the worn smooth answer skinning the oak

FOR A DRAWING

The colossus in his shoes
high hair
arms folded across chest
then the pyramid
to its squared base
and shadow

The constructed metonymy
And not the extended reformulated metaphor

And in this instance
The economy
Is molar
Not molecular

Icey eider

FURTHER

Shouting for favors with a broken nose
The seated figure stands up
And pronounces his faith in electro-magnetism
He is aware of being a prism
And applies the arrow shapes to the separate
Shadows flashing through the lacework
Of after-image and the scandals of light
Pink bread out on the gold coast
And the tilting geeks in the stillness
Who don't deserve to die standing up or between dreams
Exotic words starting to take shape in their mouths
The seated figure stands up
Coming closer an apology for debts of honor

A COAST

Coincidence
has a long
articulated arm
a frightened man
reads
for the plan
where the points flex

along the water
on the wood's border
the sunlight puts a
crisp yellow glaze
on the snowcrust

an unexpected double journey
ample and animated rites
paced by coin

firm strawberries
a piano
pages turning bite the air
brought here (taken there)
with smooth greetings

small fortune's frail music

POEM

There is something else
Made from going forward
And though the vertical
Savvy is fraudulent it is
Full of accumulated change
Days of resistance and
Order sandbagging light
With a mid-air echo mute
Reference like a principle
Embroidered with noise

THE POLITICS OF CONTRABAND

1

The plume
hunter's
timeless
bond with
the bird:
a coefficient
of restitution
generous
the golden
plumed lesser
bird of paradise
and modern roads
along the coast
and through the valley
it has plumes
then he dances

2

An ethos
of place
made

like the
armada
fooled

by the tides
and winds
laden

with much
that did
not pertain

KEWPIE B

In accord with the worst there is lustre
Quite main and by cypher the vantage of ambush
Reconstructed as feedback descendant of nostalgia
The street the choir the suck and slur of gab
The flank and file are taped to the slogans
Prospects for a cunning serenity under the arches

VIRTUOSO PEACH

Rat systems down a rope
All keening and chronology
Hand-pleat my maneuver
To put the equals in the sequels
Picking out the static
in the nickname's lavish funk
and the hint's jiggle and twist
Torque's extremely funny in solitary
All your aloha charm steeped in huge aloha charm
Fat teeth sunk in the bankrupt buzz
Philanthropy's shadow juice
Down the arm

MULBERRY 9

witness shock
    cardinal hinge
smooth does all native

of soil
the fate subject
    dark house
        always all hand

it won't be long
  what remains
    was plied
beak tap

        to music
hill learning
  new look to coins
green and cool

    poured at a
memory
        climate facts
just beyond the door

    mastery
and the herd
  the tense geometry
of the patient dog

EYELOAD AND MIRRORSTONE

Idle stunts of the iota
Zenith minor
Acumen of Thersites

What water makes hard
An alchemy of decisive grace
Winter light scratched on a ring

The copious bilge
of fast memories
traversing the humid

    Crow lift
over the octopus

Dollar guys
jumping out of chairs
on dollar days   their heads expanding
offer an umpteenth tribal lay
market hallelujah
stolen from the quiet
hump with

a struggle at a rude depth
and warble

Thumb tooth and nose

WHEN TORRID RHYMES WITH FOREHEAD

The beautiful solution
Is the rotate and build-up
A hurricane beat just to stay alive
That part of the action
That goes through the window
Arms crossed over the eyes
Crisscross salt with the big music
And no one knows the stranger's face
A nice hat though and a surge
In the ear
          Here's where
When the tough get going
The weird get wired
Saxophones rough with the dervish loons
And oracle sports short-cut
The harmonies and technicians
Only put electricity in the cardboard
But meeting the expectations
Of humor's restraint
Is a proton event not
Eternity's gas leak
               The fat name
Returned in the lion's mouth
Hero foam and
Hot legs sharp shirts coats off
And it looks like it
Won't have to rain for a while
And there'll be a whole lot of music
Before anyone gets knocked down

Tim Tom Jocko Bill Ted Larry Fred Mike
Al Burt John Dale Chuck George Mel Joe
We're all watching the ghosts
Back in the long long ago

FIVE

TERRITORY

I

The desperado
and his abacus
in utopia
        he plays
a white enamel
saxophone
and she
wears a dark
blue dress

II

pollen pigment
the real impulse of periphery
knotted in speech
like death
fear's magic lethargy

distraction's lead wafer
on the tongue shapes duration
and the fact of memory
its status in the proposition
its purpose in the process
intentional poise
over legible shifting proportion

agreement makes systems
if you weren't so readily amused
more people would respect you
frustration tags your vowel sounds
and your consonants distribute a fiction
like a manipulated photograph

prompt random and common
scanning tracking blocking
advance bounded the distinctive natural order
graph tick focus fumble wave
current distracted late lateral
coaxed combed shook counted

in the mercury lair
a hive

III

low light makes a landscape
out of distance

a poem is one of the almost successful
forces of nature

smacked around by repetition and
reflection

electric calendar and ancient alphabet
ferocious but hybrid specifications

ringing the changes on the mythology
of riff

point where the point runs to and back again
the rigors of function and novelty

passage mechanics shagging the circular
angle by angle one secret or the next

perfecting the transparent source
indolent strut dithering at the meridian

or just hammering at the window
a preserved disclosure something skeletal

fortuitous and taut

IV

a plump and
torpid atom
sweats

instinct's
verdict
sustains an

aphorism
soft bullet
rolled against

the signal
motion's membrane
small candid and *mach*

V

white animals
in the dark
red trees

footsteps
a tradition
squandered

in silence
colors fade on
the tins of dust

when the apple
danced with the piepan
gone sepia and yellow

surfaces all
contrition to make
synchrony a blunder

counterpoint arrested
hand held deep
in the peach powder

of corruption
thum thum thum
it sounds in the dark

VI

eyes building a sun
a dog tied to the tongue

the consolations of winter
sustained by roots and the harmonies
of slowest change

lambent cycles for light
clenched by a sharp angle

making a new proportion
by jumping on the blood
like a nomad with his last word

intrepid menace tickles the arch
in the step by step

an energy that shoulders the empty
reminds the coherent in its lair
of no rainbow meridian

how laughter is found maimed by
the passivity that maintains its own discourse

VII

penny paper acoustic research
dinner with a lawyer
wake up hungry in the bushes
penny paper acoustic research
dinner with a lawyer
what's the word jumped on first
penny paper acoustic research
dinner with a lawyer
transparent margins and a balcony
penny paper acoustic research
dinner with a lawyer
named Schoolhouse or Postman
penny paper acoustic research
dinner with a lawyer
mandarin piping murky affection
penny paper
acoustic research
habitat for soup
has been a has been
now has a seat and
a point of view
that would rest
in a perspective
appropriate to a short menu
fragile suggestions
Byzantine exhaustions
penny paper
acoustic research
obstinate

scrubbed of custom
no pictures for the music
but many peddlers
rough-out with voices
the corner to corner
dispensing a synthesis of discretion
and an intoxicating uncertainty
penny paper
acoustic research
insert adapt shuffle and dance

VIII

a light that builds forms
a light that dissolves them
the mechanical planet
intentions silver and ebony
sealed in a ball of ice
the big picture
everywhere and meantime
grief is pneumatic
ravers fill the aisles
stat stump notch
stat st-stat stat st-stat
product

IX

The zero
is glass grey
a bark sharp
in the spine
the one cued
particle pierces
the cipher
whose glyph
for instinct
is part of
the rational
ceremony
the extremities
of approval
leech and
replicate
a hole
attached
to a pattern
the sun's shade

X

urban
curving
dumb
clay

risk
assaults
the proud
noise

wind
on the paint
fresh white
sound

attic
joists
static
seams

inter-
vention
elbow
eye

tri-
angle
frantic
triangular

XI

Whose
(menace
à trois)
shabby
illusions
(whose
((absolute))
mistaken
outline
whose
proper
argument
makes it
(((menace
à trois)))
absolute)
and so
mortar
the sub-
conscious
lessons
menace
à trois:
I give
you
this
but count
your
fingers

the triangle
is a menace
one with two
for three
that's
you holding
it minus
a digit
or more
plus
this

XII

The perpendicular
and forgotten
the accumulated
extracted and scratched
proportion paced
from the diorama
a lens replaces
the small aperture
a tight fit but
it stretches to accomodate
the truncated and
indifferent peg of light
what he says
he sees
        a sleek yes
the perpendicular has
its reach for refuge
but is forgotten with
the accumulated
extracted and scratched
see what he says

XIII

hard to the north
hard to the south
and east a wilderness
maunders
           to the west
canaille technicians
make excavations
in the sounds they make

in the east
the fortuitous
is in suspense
this is untrue
but evocative

in the west
the fortuitous
is a can of worms
this is not untrue
but expedient

in the west nose
is put to ear
in the east ear
is pressed to ear
for discourse

so inconsequential
a dynamic—derelict
in its mastery of
distinction—it self-
corrects and bleeds water

soon a bay forms
where the preposterous
and formal splash and flounder
but in the east a sinister
charm hangs in the ear—loud and still

XIV

mid-June the glare
wheeling over the wreckage
a breeze camouflages
a hazard the bruise and
matter-of-fact is tropical
a sympathy of bright blue for orange
for vigilance and a privilege
of words
        sophisticated aptitude
of the solitary
saxophone gusts pledge up the rambunctious
measure
        a legacy of themes and intervals

XV

Light, temperature, and time of day.
The rain falls straight down filling
the courtyard with a more supple silence
and emptiness. The morning is strewn with
beautiful sentences that hold a few of the
less necessary things in place but who am
I to judge, the lingo wallah of Chelsea
in a Palm Beach suit, Panama hat with a
feather headband, soft canvas shoes—
a regular guy whose recent guests have
included a purveyor of ancient dictionaries
and those who keep bread on their table by
carrying air conditioners up and down stairs . . .
and a tile man who once was Al Pacino's chauffeur.
We talk about Al, Marty Bregman, Oliver Stone.
Gritslish, gritslish, gritslish goes the grout.
Light, temperature, and time of day.
The rain falls straight down filling
the courtyard with beautiful unnecessary
sentences making the silence more supple.

XVI

Modulation of the gradual
and orotund

How many fingers
should I hold in front of you

To provoke a soft eccentricity
gallant and irrational

And far stronger than the tradition
provoked by the learned meta-comrade

Clear source of the obscure element
incalculably backward

A rainbow from right to left
rising & forfeit in the silence

XVII

the work shoots along
planting the end breaks
nearer the eyes or
between the eyes
exhales guesswork
the diamond magnet
works side to side
the invisible postulates
and a secret that's safe
with me casts a shadow
a million miles across
your face bubbles of
direction eyes ears nose
and mouth and a voice
that pumps the angles
the day before yesterday
still ripples leap the limit
all razor luck and wizard twist

XVIII

white shirt

panther's heart

nothing at all

a black scrawl

full sail

one two
three
two one

three (got)
from here
and here to there

this is it there
they are
the five

arm against
the wall
the scrub of brick

vapor trail
and window glare
piano tar and chalk

XIX

the stick man
grins
he lopes and
strides
        the stick
man tells all
the stick man
is not eternally
young
        he tells me
he's come to
realize this
the stick man
shows tears
through his
bi-focals
an important
measure
to the stick
man is when
tears come
to the eyes
how the stick
man brought
tears to
the eyes
of any the stick
man speaks
of his heroic

brittleness
and its cold
stiff angles
of access
to any tears
it can bring
soothing
the stick man
and the wooden
pulse of his
measure

XX

mirage or moan point
an obscure route carved by inches
a gull against the far reaches of projection
isolated gestures like fading shadows
the sleep of choice between the hungry comfort
and the art it shapes   *che brutta gente*
the shrug in the branch that turns the light

indignation wrestles a stump exactly awkward
but the yield is time
and illusion's feature regret
how it is how it drags attention
to where assigned conviction squats
pins and flags in a ripe peach
while in the green cabaña a small ticking sound
arranges the damage
tight bulge and shuffle go like a dance
boom monkey at the traps
and I like his brim
it cuts the light my way

XXI

skids per cubic rag
check the distance

extrapolate some resonance
a specimen (cool dark alley)

check the distance
flash transit (American made)

negotiate the skids
register the specimen

coin of the realm
per cubic rag (long distance poke)

original admission
you're brought in on it

extrapolate the distance
lens scratched (it still lines up)

glow job (primal and profuse)
fanatic spiral (cannibal of essentials)

the nervous ritual contracts
into reputation

to do with it
south sauce (blood) and the subtle mumble

XXII

eye odd
the nimble cargo
parasites rich
in the highsign

odd eye
grudge freight
heavy shadows
between small patches of light

webs of dust
steam and rust
for fortune's
second wind

XXIII

Persuasive solitude
rosies the intelligence
Flamingoes for fingers
and a broken foot
Luck darts the length
of the dry ditch and back
It had to try something
No telling what would
happen next—the maroon
egg of revenge caught in the throat

XXIV

remote unison
prismatic and
dissolving in
the grapple a
sense of sake
engaging calm
and a loss of
an equivalent
where the sum
gives contour
with thirteen
pulls to cull
a sonnet from
sparks of ink
Webster's tar

XXV

money makes an outside
the oddly equated division
like a parcel of land
fenced by a category of trees
and broken fence that share
a record of folly—cockeyed
and frantic in its origins
and retarded by access and cash

a scrap of correction
fiercest when the words are cold
and the white that stark
sepulchral blank holding
the sameness that amazes the world
presumption turned to sawdust
a line of sight an extended moment
small dots between the letters
balanced midway on the vertical
isolate the secure tether
and lock the horizontal
title only as deep as the accent

XXVI

the account
big chemistry
for prosper

thorns dissolved
in ink and sweat
big chemistry

tells the account
for prosper
primitive tracing

first ritual
scorch naked and
separate on a dark wall

trusting the soot
of big chemistry
for prosper in

firelight that tempers
and coaxes first a
hand then a hot wing

traced in the fault
an account for the eyes
head first not

of words or ear
but brief lambent
ochre rays

dark prosper
big chemistry
ink tooth or horn

from account
to chronicle
and tract

XXVII

irked lot in big coats
and fat leather chairs
all jake torpedo artisans
cultivating predicaments
wild and dreadful they
size-up with a knuckle-ear
calculus . . . imposing
silk clumsy jackals
cuff the coin

XXVIII

Impeding criminal justice
and testing the pleasure place
three bald men in wet coats stand
around a machine that only minutes
before exploded into a
million pieces—re- or de- defined
but X now marks the spot
(0161-032-06321OK) dabbles in
the alchemy of forever and a day
ONE WRITES IN HIS NOTEBOOK
ANOTHER WALKS AROUND AND LOOKS
AT AS MANY PIECES LITTERING THE ROOM
AS HE CAN AND THE OTHER
STANDS IN A CORNER AND REMEMBERS
HOW ON VARIOUS OCCASIONS OVER THE YEARS
HE HAD PUT COINS INTO THE RE- OR DE-
DEFINED MACHINE AND WAITED FOR HIS
COLD DRINK AND CHANGE BUT THEY HAD
NEVER MATERIALIZED AND HOW HE HAD
PRESSED HIS EAR TO THE MACHINE AND FELT
IT COLD ON HIS CHEEK WHILE HE LISTENED
TO THE SOFT HUM AND CLICK HUM AND CLICK
WHILE THE MINUTES PASSED

                        THE ONE WHO
REMEMBERED OWED MONEY TO THE ONE WHO
WROTE IN HIS NOTEBOOK THE ONE WHO WALKED
AROUND LOOKING AT THE MANY PIECES OWED
SOMETHING—IT WASN'T MONEY AND IT WASN'T

HIS LIFE—TO THE ONE WHO REMEMBERED BUT IT WAS AN IMPEDIMENT AND WHILE THEY WROTE LOOKED AND REMEMBERED THE SUN WENT DOWN AND THE MOON CAME UP AND THE RAIN BEGAN TO FALL THE LOCKSMITH ARRIVED AND AFTER HIM A LYNCH MOB AND AFTER THEM THE SAVAGE GOD

XXIX

Tangent's rigor

wedges the ankle

useful muttering

determines the

dissolve's pace

deftly anaesthetic

How it will tell

the oyster's roof

over the purely

speculative knot

transfigured layers

plum of the tides

XXX

a confused solution
emerges stranded
from the ceremony

a confused solution
puts a better light
on the overflow

a confused solution
shoulder to shoulder
shifting the charms

a confused solution
persists however
solemn the maxims

a confused solution
ripens the adage
an almost natural moment

a confused solution
threaded therefore
to therefore

a confused solution
figures into the gibbet
or signposts of a measured tone

a confused solution
the side-effects of fidelity
at odd moments

a confused solution
orchestrated and taut
registers an outline

a confused solution
floats like a compass
in oil like a compass

XXXI

A pause attached to the sense of wear
starts the pattern of rhyme
behind the ear
              peeling off the shine
flint records
           still ringing
the bright chips scattered through the yellow light
contemplation's manufacture
stinging the eye with the dust that flies
through the blunder
spearhead was a hammerhead
diverts the bird muscle
with a wave of glory thumb to palm
the wrist's bias all argument
the wordless distance point to feather
and heart
              no comfort describes the fear

XXXII

The balk was dead fresh
and ephemeral when it
caught the blinking booed
The balk was dead fresh
but it kept on moving
along like the wizard
of walk and postponed
legato while hoot-hooting
the overwrought who
could only jaw the echo
and glare—dud frenzy
in the cheap seats with
less than a minute left
The balk was dead fresh
a spasm, a quaver hemmed
by the blowing dust but
hanging in the eye was
a zigzag jerking the high
kick into an apparatus
run on a fuckup cold
raver in a brouhaha should
have gone with the flow

XXXIII

In its corruption only the buried plan
survives—an apology to inspection
undefined to convictions of use—
infinite calibrations of darkness
the shadows of passing cars against
the ceiling exaggerated, persuasive,
a quarry of wakefulness—an argument's
path run to stone and painted glass.

Threadbare and attractive the frayed puzzle
is frozen in its emphasis—a ridge of muted
but ingenious salutations to the contrary
who scramble and bark in the vacuum of their questions.
The evasive is registered, the patient legend
reconfined to the ordinary where real life
regroups its discreet revelations according
to a plan of paper-thin moods and surprises.

XXXIV

rags and riddles
labor a point
for consolation
think of running

speak of the wreck
speak to the wreck
compression's shelter
prompt crisscrossing

farming the mislaid
amiable tags locking
on a salutation from
different directions

until the tongue
turns blue
consonance impossible
out hunting a cramp in the grace

harmonies quieted in
the mirrored variety
stumped profit the host
tone obdurate and still

eager and embracing any
rebuke piping or aggregate
assemblage reviving the initial
delirium thumb skid through oblivion

XXXV

brag rooted
  bragroot
    rage
mud on the ear

thinking wholeness
answered by
          rendered
bragroot
rage
    pulled
cut in the fire

history lotus decay
wicker verb
steady as the air
under the wing
          endures
the foolish wind
arterial
to concur

brood
of the brute
emphatic dwarf
blunt torch
in the fist

rubric veining

the clepsydra
azure botch
and toothprint
marring
        bragroot
inked

RAY DI PALMA

Born in New Kensington, Pennsylvania in 1943, Ray DiPalma received his undergraduate education at Duquesne University and an M.F.A. from the University of Iowa. After graduate school he combined college teaching in the mid-west with extensive travel in Europe until 1975, when he settled with his wife, the artist Elizabeth DiPalma, in New York City.

He began writing in the late 1950s and published his first work in magazines in 1962. His first book, *Max*, appeared in 1969. In the early 1970s he edited a series of literary magazines and published a number of books by poets who were later to be associated with so-called Language writing. Also included in the pages of these magazines were early translations (by such now well-known writers as Paul Auster and Rosmarie and Keith Waldrop) of French poets of the stature of Claude Royet-Journoud, Jacques Dupin, and Jean Follain.

By 1973 he had started creating visual and written works that were, in part, intended to extend the notion of textual images. Among these visual works are one-of-a-kind artist's books, sound texts, collages and prints. Publications include *The Sargasso Transcries* (1974), *Marquee* (1977), *Genesis* (1980), *Labyrinth Radio* (1981), and *Startle Luna* (1984). In Berlin in 1982 Edition Vogelsang published two collections of his graphic works, *Dreizehn Arbeiten* and *Dreiundzwanzig Arbeiten*. Over the years his visual works have appeared in numerous group exhibitions in the United States, Europe, South America, and Japan as well as in a one-man show in Amsterdam. Many of these pieces are now in public and private collections. DiPalma's recent work in this area encompasses sculpture and assemblage as well as computer-generated text and image.

In 1978 Sun & Moon Press published his *Cuiva Sails*. A series of highly formal and stylized works were to follow. Among these strikingly different writings are *Planh* (1979), *Two Poems* (1982), *January Zero* (1984) (a poem which first appeared in the journal *Sun & Moon*), and *Raik* (1989). His widely-anthologized prose work *January Zero* has recently appeared in a French translation by

Emmanuel Hocquard and in 1991 was the subject of a video created by the young French writer and artist Justine Adenis. Current projects have included a book-length sequence of poems written by DiPalma in French entitled *Rue de Tanger* as well as a forthcoming collaboration with the European artist Alexandre Delay.

DiPalma has received fellowships from the National Endowment for the Arts and the New York State Council on the Arts. And in 1991, as part of a series sponsored by the Foundation Royaumont, he gave readings in Paris, Bordeaux and Grenoble.

Unafraid to draw on past literary traditions as well as to create a very personal and unique tradition of its own, DiPalma has for more than twenty years written work that has defied easy classification. The poems collected in *Numbers and Tempers* (selected from numerous early collections and limited editions now out of print) reveal a sensibility at once lyrical as well as fiercely experimental—even hieratic. DiPalma's fine ear and sharp eye are consistently apparent throughout. And these writings reveal his capacity, from the start, to express the power and variety of language's substantive immediacy.

SUN & MOON CLASSICS

Sun & Moon Classics is a publicly supported nonprofit program to publish new editions and translations or republications of outstanding world literature of the late nineteenth and twentieth centuries. Organized by The Contemporary Arts Educational Project, Inc., a nonprofit corportation, and published by its program Sun & Moon Press, the series is made possible, in part, by grants and individual contributions.

This book was made possible, in part, through a matching grant from the California Arts Council, the Cultural Affairs Department of the City of Los Angeles, through a grant from The Andrew W. Mellon Foundation. The following individuals have made contributions to this Series and/or to the Project.

Kathy Acker (San Francisco, California)
Tom Ahern (Warwick, Rhode Island)
Charles Altieri (Seattle, Washington)
John Arden (Galway, Ireland)
Paul Auster (Brooklyn, New York)
Dennis Barone (West Hartford, Connecticut)
Jonathan Baumbach (Brooklyn, New York)
In Memoriam: Juan Benet
Steve Benson (Berkeley, California)
Bill Berkson (Bolinas, California)
Charles Bernstein (New York, New York)
Sherry Bernstein (New York, New York)
George Bowering (Vancouver, Canada)
Christine Brooke-Rose (Paris, France)
In Memoriam: John Cage
Ernesto Cardenal (Managua, Nicaragua)
William Corbett (Boston, Massachusetts)
Robert Crosson (Los Angeles, California)
Tina Darragh and P. Inman (Greenbelt, Maryland)
Fielding Dawson (New York, New York)
Henri Deluy (Jury-sur-Seine, France)
Christopher Dewdney (Toronto, Canada)
Arkadii Dragomoschenko (St. Petersburg, Russia)

In Memoriam: Phillip Dunne
George Economou (Norman, Oklahoma)
Richard Elman (Stony Brook, New York)
Kenward Elmslie (Calais, Vermont)
Elaine Equi and Jerome Sala (New York, New York)
Lawrence Ferlinghetti (San Francisco, California)
Richard Foreman (New York, New York)
Howard N. Fox (Los Angeles, California)
Jerry Fox (Aventura, Florida)
In Memoriam: Rose Fox
Melvyn Freilicher (San Diego, California)
Allen Ginsberg (New York, New York)
Peter Glassgold (Brooklyn, New York)
Barbara Guest (New York, New York)
Perla and Amiram V. Karney (Bel Air, California)
Fred Haines (Los Angeles, California)
Fanny Howe (La Jolla, California)
Vaclav Havel (Prague, The Czech Republic)
Ruth Prawer Jhabvala (New York, New York)
Harold Jaffe (San Diego, California)
Ira S. Jaffe (Albuquerque, New Mexico)
Alex Katz (New York, New York)
Steve Katz (Boulder, Colorado)
Tom LaFarge (New York, New York)
Norman Lavers (Jonesboro, Arkansas)
Herbert Lust (Greenwich, Connecticut)
Harry Mathews (Paris France)
Norman MacAffee (New York, New York)
In Memoriam: Mary McCarthy
Rosemary Macchiavelli (Washington, D.C.)
In Memoriam: John Mandanis
Harry Mulisch (Amsterdam, The Netherlands)
Iris Murdoch (Oxford, England)
In Memoriam: bp nichol
Toby Olson (Philadelphia, Pennsylvania)
Maggie O'Sullivan (Hebden Bridge, England)
Rochelle Owens (Norman, Oklahoma)
Ron Padgett (New York, New York)
Marjorie and Joseph Perloff (Pacific Palisades, California)
Dennis Phillips (Culver City, California)
Carl Rakosi (San Francisco, California)
Tom Raworth (Cambridge, England)

David Reed (New York, New York)
Ishmael Reed (Oakland, California)
Janet Rodney (Santa Fe, New Mexico)
Diane and Jerome Rothenberg (Encinatas, California)
Dr. Marvin and Ruth Sackner (Miami Beach, Florida)
Floyd Salas (Berkeley, California)
Tom Savage (New York, New York)
Leslie Scalapino (Oakland, California)
Aaron Shurin (San Francisco, California)
Charles Simic (Strafford, New Hampshire)
Gustaf Sobin (Goult, France)
Gilbert Sorrentino (Stanford, California)
Catharine R. Stimpson (Staten Island, New York)
Ronald Sukenick (Boulder, Colorado)
John Taggart (Newburg, Pennsylvania)
Nathaniel Tarn (Tesque, New Mexico)
Fiona Templeton (New York, New York)
Mitch Tuchman (Los Angeles, California)
Keith and Rosmarie Waldrop (Providence, Rhode Island)
Anne Walter (Carnac, France)
Mac Wellman (New York, New York)
Arnold Wesker (Hay on Wye, England)
C. D. Wright (Barrington, Rhode Island)

Douglas Messerli
Publisher, Sun & Moon Press
Director, The Contemporary Arts Educational Project, Inc.

If you would like to be a contributor to this series, please send
your tax-deductible contribution to The Contemporary Arts Educational
Project, Inc., a non-profit corporation, 6026 Wilshire Boulevard,
Los Angeles, California 90036

Selected SUN & MOON CLASSICS and other internationally-acclaimed publications.

All titles are published in paperback unless otherwise noted.

Bruce Andrews [USA]
  Give Em Enough Rope ($10.95)
  I Don't Have Any Paper So Shut Up ($13.95)
David Antin [USA]
  Selected Poems: 1963-1973 ($13.95)
Paul Auster [USA]
  The Art of Hunger: Essays-Prefaces-Interviews
    (cloth, $24.95)
  *The New York Trilogy [City of Glass,
    Ghosts,* and *The Locked Room]* (cloth, $27.95)
Russell Banks [USA]
  Family Life (cloth, $13.95)
  The Relation of My Imprisonment (cloth, $12.95)
Djuna Barnes [USA]
  The Book of Repulsive Women ($5.00)
  Interviews ($12.95)
  New York ($13.95)
  Smoke and Other Early Stories ($9.95)
Charles Bernstein [USA]
  Content's Dream: Essays 1975-1984 ($14.95)
  The Nude Formalism [with Susan Bee] ($5.00)
  Rough Trades ($10.95)
  The Sophist ($11.95)
Jens Bjorneboe [NORWAY]
  The Bird Lovers (forthcoming)
André Breton [FRANCE]
  Earthlight ($12.95)
David Bromige [CANADA]
  The Harbor Master of Hong Kong ($10.95)
Clark Coolidge [USA]
  Own Face (forthcoming)
  The Rova Improvisations ($11.95)
  Solution Passage: Poems 1978-1981 ($11.95)
  Sound As Thought ($11.95)

Ray DiPalma [USA]
  Mock Fandago ($5.00)
  Numbers and Tempers: Selected Early Poems ($11.95)
Heimito von Doderer [AUSTRIA]
  The Demons ($29.95)
Arkadii Dragomoschenko [RUSSIA]
  Description ($11.95)
  Xenia ($12.95)
Dominique Fourcade [FRANCE]
  xbo (forthcoming)
Sigmund Freud [AUSTRIA] (see also Wilhelm Jensen)
  Delusion and Dream in Jensen's Gradiva ($13.95)
Barbara Guest [USA]
  Defensive Rapture ($11.95)
  Fair Realism (cloth, $13.95)
Marianne Hauser [USA]
  Me & My Mom! ($9.95)
  The Memoirs of the Late Mr. Ashley ($11.95)
  Prince Ishmael ($11.95)
Lyn Hejinian [USA]
  The Cell ($11.95)
  My Life ($9.95)
Fanny Howe [USA]
  The Deep North ($9.95)
  The Lives of a Spirit (cloth, $10.95)
  Saving History ($12.95)
Susan Howe [USA]
  The Europe of Trusts ($10.95)
Wilhelm Jensen [GERMANY] (see also Sigmund Freud)
  Gradiva ($13.95)
Steve Katz [USA]
  Florry of Washington Heights ($10.95)
  43 Fictions ($12.95)
  Weir & Pouce ($10.95)
Valery Larbaud [FRANCE]
  Childish Things ($13.95)
Jackson Mac Low [USA]
  Pieces O' Six ($11.95)
F. T. Marinetti [ITALY]
  Let's Murder the Moonshine ($13.95)
  The Untameables ($10.95)
José Emilio Pacheco [MEXICO]
  A Distant Death (forthcoming)

Michael Palmer [USA]
  First Figure (NORTH POINT PRESS, $8.50)
  Notes for Echo Lake (NORTH POINT PRESS, $9.95)
  Sun (NORTH POINT PRESS, $9.95)
Tom Raworth [ENGLAND]
  Eternal Sections ($9.95)
Leslie Scalapino [USA]
  Defoe (forthcoming)
  Considering how exaggerated music is
    (NORTH POINT PRESS, $10.95)
  Crowd and not evening or light
    (O BOOKS/SUN & MOON PRESS, $9.00)
  that they were at the beach
    (NORTH POINT PRESS, $9.50)
  way (NORTH POINT PRESS, $12.00)
Arthur Schnitzler [AUSTRIA]
  Dream Story ($10.95)
  Lieutenant Gustl ($9.95)
Gertrude Stein [USA]
  Mrs. Reynolds ($11.95)
  Stanzas in Meditation (forthcoming)
  Tender Buttons ($9.95)
Stijn Streuvels [BELGIUM/FLANDERS]
  The Flaxfield ($11.95)
Italo Svevo [ITALY]
  As a Man Grows Older ($12.95)
Carl Van Vechten [USA]
  Parties ($13.95)
Tarjei Vesaas [NORWAY]
  The Ice Palace ($11.95)
Wendy Walker [USA]
  The Sea-Rabbit ($11.95)
  The Secret Service ($13.95)
Mac Wellman [USA]
  Theatre of Wonders (ed.) ($10.95)

Individuals may order books directly from:
SUN & MOON PRESS
6026 Wilshire Boulevard
Los Angeles, California 90036
(213) 857-1115